I remember finding myself in a season of a type of "spiritual rut," and it seemed to be triggered the more when I heard various speakers talk in context to relationship with the Lord. I felt as though I was missing something, but I couldn't seem to put my finger on it, but as Minister Johnnie Prophet expounded upon the importance of fellowship, it was like my spirit leaped within me and at that moment I knew that Holy Spirit had delivered to me the missing key to my quest for closer intimacy with the Lord.

—KELVIN STEELE SR., PASTOR OF ABBA
FATHER CHURCH OF FAITH

When I heard this message from Brother Prophet, it took a minute for it to sink into my spirit but when it did, this is what it revealed; many of us are walking around in a relationship with God, thinking we are good, but in reality, we are missing out on the things God has for us because we are really just in ourselves. When we realize that fellowshipping with God brings us closer to Him and we really get to know who God is, that real intimacy with Him, that's what He desires with us and will allow God to show you what he has for our life!

—KEITH MILLS, MINISTER FRIEND

Relationship to Fellowship

Special Comments about
RELATIONSHIP TO FELLOWSHIP

A church plight? Allowing just a relationship with Jesus Christ is a believer's and a church's plight. True, a relationship with Christ is required to be a believer in Christ, but for many it is merely a "connection" with the Savior. To many, it is only a link with the Divine—a hookup that provides eternal security. In Johnnie's writings, he brings to our attention the desire of the Lord, for us who belong to the Godhead, that we make an "investment" in our relationship. That's fellowship. While "relationship" is an interconnection between the individual and Christ, "fellowship" is an interconnection—and an investment of sharing together— between the believer and Christ. Johnnie writes of the different facets of the desired investment Christ wants for us. Prepare yourself for revelation.

—DR. JIM PICKENS, APOSTLE, HOUSE OF FAITH

Fellowship is a refreshing new word that is actually very old. We have spent most of our lives developing a relationship with Father God rather than fellowship. When Johnnie began to share from his heart the deep need for fellowship that God was sharing with him, it resonated in my spirit. I began to deliberately seek Father God for developing my fellowship with Him even more. I discovered during our times of fellowship that He shares His heart with me. He shares His desires for me. It has brought my relationship with Him to a whole new level, a whole new meaning. Now mind you, we talked before and He shared things with me before, but there is something different now. It has made a "new me" in this venture with Him. It has opened more of the prophetic. I invite you to open your heart to God as you read this book that Holy Spirit has given to Prophet Johnnie. Allow Him to soar within you.

—APOSTLE PAT PICKENS

As I consider how important fellowship with the Father is, Holy Spirit reminded me of a tradition I attempted to start with my son. It felt as though we were going in separate spiritual directions. The prospect of the two of us spending time together, I presumed, would offer an environment of trust and openness for both of us to share those heartfelt matters/emotions as it pertained to our God, family, friends, and each other. Thanks be to Almighty God; I discovered my son and I had so much in common. Through this precious time with my son, all defenses were removed quickly because of love. Holy Spirit reminded me of the wonderful times my son and I spent together when he was younger. I drove him to school most days and picked him up. We spent many hours watching planes take off on the air force base and often listened to our former pastor's preaching tapes as we drove home . . . we were in close fellowship. Because we did not maintain our fellowship, we experienced more of a relationship without fellowship. I would see him at church and/or Sunday dinner, without much communication or should I say fellowship. Recently, circumstances in his life changed, which resulted in a spiritual change. It caused my son to desire a greater fellowship with God and drew us closer again. The significance of this story is fellowship is a foundational key to a fortified, meaningful relationship. The focus scripture in James 4:8, "draw nigh to God and He will draw nigh to you," lends its truth to our familial and personal relationships. The more time we spend in fellowship with each other, the stronger the relational bond positively intensifies. It starts with us strengthening and nurturing the need to fellowship with Yahweh.

—GREG ANDERSON, SR. PASTOR, THE ROCK OF TAMPA BAY

Relationship

— to —

Fellowship

Second Edition

*The grace of the Lord Jesus Christ and the love of God
and the fellowship of the Holy Spirit be with you all.*

2 CORINTHIANS 13:14 (ESV)

JOHNNIE O. PROPHET

RELATIONSHIP TO FELLOWSHIP MINISTRIES INC.
Brooksville, Florida

Published by Relationship to Fellowship Ministries Inc.

PO Box 9004
Brooksville, FL 34604

www.relationshiptofellowship.com

Cover and Interior Design by Imagine! Studios
www.ArtsImagine.com

Cover Image: iStock.com/freedom007

ISBN: 979-8-9877186-0-5
Library of Congress Control Number: 2023933050

First Edition 2020, Second Edition 2023
First Printing: February 2023

TABLE OF CONTENTS

SPECIAL THANK YOU

To my wife, Jerlyn Prophet, for encouraging me to continue to press in to know and fulfill God's purpose for my being.

And to my siblings, Emily Shelley, Darren Davis, and Valarie Grace, for the many times they, too, encouraged me to answer the call of God and to walk therein.

INTRODUCTION

Moving from Relationship to Fellowship in my thinking has changed how I view God, His Kingdom, His Church, my wife, my family, and the world. Fellowship makes and solidifies relationships.

Born a Boy—Desired to Be a Son

Several years ago, I thought much about what I may have missed out on by not having my dad in my life while growing up. (I will comment more on this later.) My mother had to raise six children without a father in the home. What and who she had was a mother, my grandmother Essie Prophet, whom we called Big Momma. Big Momma stepped in to help when she could, and what a major role she played in sowing the Gospel seed in the lives of me and three of my siblings. As a little boy, for about three years while me and my siblings lived with Big Momma, she kept us in church, twice on Sunday (morning service and evening service), on Wednesdays, and most Fridays. I must admit, I did not like having to go to church so much. But little did I know, God used that time spent with her to plant the seed of His word and kingdom in me that would years later be watered by other saints of God, with God giving increase to it. Thank you, Lord.

When I was a child, my biological father was not in my life. I wanted so much to have a relationship with him, but that never materialized. Once, when I was around twenty-three years of age, one of his siblings gave me his phone number. He lived in a different city and state than we did. I called the number. Sure enough, he answered the phone. I told him who I was and that my family and I were flying to Europe and had a layover in the city where he lived and that I would love to meet with him, if only for a short time. He explained he did not want to meet with me. He said he wanted me to live my life and let him live his. We never met. I thought, at least I heard his voice. I never heard his voice again. I often wondered what he could have imparted to me as my father and what kind of blessing I could have been to him. After all, he was my dad, relative, family. And yet I never heard his voice again. I believe a man can make a child and never be a father. Likewise, a child can be born and never became a true son or daughter. To become such requires capturing and respecting each other's hearts, hence fellowship.

For years, I often thought on that brief phone conversation, wondering what could have been if he had met with me. Note: a father can be in the home and not have fellowship with his son. I can see where I may have, at times, faltered in this to some degree.

Another time I experience this difference was in 2014, when I attended a cousin's NFL draft day party. While in attendance, Holy Spirit instructed me to observe my soon-to-be-drafted cousin's actions with the many family members that were present at the party. What I saw helped me understand more of what Holy Spirit was teaching me. Holy Spirit asked me, "Do you see how many of the family members he merely greeted and kept it moving without any dialogue, but with a few he really engaged with smiles and enjoyment, holding extensive conversations?" He had engaging communication (fellowship) with them. I then realized the family members he had extensive communion with that they had spent quality time with him over the years and were in constant communication. In all, a good 95 percent of the attendees at the NFL draft day party were his relatives. To his mother, he was a son, to his grandmother, a grandson. He was a brother to his siblings, a nephew to his aunts and uncles, and to others, like me, a cousin. It was a family full of relationships.

I didn't have as much interaction (fellowship) with him as I did with other family members, those I talked with the most. Others I had spent little time with over the years, and when we did talk, we had little to say to each other. When you fellowship, you always have something to say to each other.

He seemed very comfortable with the ones he had an extensive conversation with. It was apparent he knew them, and they knew him. The other family members, he knew of them, and they knew of him (they'd heard of his football accomplishments), but he showed no extended fellowship with them.

Heavenly Father spoke to me several years later as I pondered not having an opportunity to know my dad. Holy Spirit began teaching me about relationship and fellowship and how different the two are. It wasn't until that day when I attended my cousin's NFL draft day party that Holy Spirt gave more clarity.

Holy Spirit showed me the difference between relationship and fellowship. I held onto hope for years, wanting very much to have my dad in my life. He was my relative. The moment I was born, the relationship between me and my dad began and never ended. Holy Spirit explained that what I really wanted was fellowship. Even while my dad was not in my life, relationally, we were still connected (related naturally—father and son).

After hearing this, I looked in various versions of the Bible (King James, New King James, New International Version, Complete Jewish Bible) and found no scriptures regarding having a relationship with God. However, I did find scriptures on fellowshipping with Him. And I came across phrases like "know Him," "seek Him," "live in and walk in Him or His Spirit."

Yes, what I wanted and needed from my biological father was more than a relationship; I needed and wanted fellowship with him.

Family reunions (relationships) seem to be about gathering to fellowship with family members, some of whom you may not have seen in years. I remember the joy of those reunion get-togethers.

What I've learned from Holy Spirit, recalling my growing up time without my dad but wanting such, and my observation of my cousin's interactions with family (relatives), is that you can have a relationship and never enter a place of fellowship.

I believe a healthy relationship must be one of fellowship. In other words, a relationship must lead into a place of fellowship—and remain to the benefit and blessing of all.

Within fellowship, you share deep affections with the other person. You can have relationships with people without ever having any genuine affection for them (my dad for me). But fellowship is something altogether different.

Purpose

Holy Spirit is so amazing. He used my desire for what I thought I wanted with my dad "relationship" to teach me of the importance and benefits of having consistent "fellowship" with God through Him (Holy Spirit). This experience has brought understanding and illumination of certain scriptures, and even revelation. My experience with Holy Spirit walking me through the difference has been a wonderful journey, which has affected my heart, mind and spirit and has caused me to look forward to what Holy Spirit will continue to do in and through me for the Glory of God.

By Holy Spirit, I will use this word "fellowship" throughout the pages of this book, using the examples of men mentioned in the Bible with whom God had fellowship as they fellowshipped with Him.

I do not intend to split hairs as I share what I have learned about the differences between relationship and fellowship through my walk with Holy Spirit, attending to His showing me how the two words' meanings differ. Understanding this difference has changed how I read scripture ('graphe—graf-ay', Strong's #1124). Graphe is defined as a drawing, a painting, a writing). As I read the Holy Scriptures through the eyes of fellowship, I seek the mind and intent of the One in whom the Holy Scriptures point me to, the One I am to honor and worship, "the Personal and manifested Word" ('logos', Strong's #3056). Doing so has often helped me enter a place where I can hear the spoken word ('rhema', Strong's #4487), with the desire to obey fully the one in whom Holy Spirit inspired writers of the written word to speak of, Jesus.

"You search the Scriptures ('graphe') for in them you think you have eternal life; and these are they which testify of Me" (John 5:39).

"Now all these things happened to them as examples, and they were 'written' for our admonition, upon whom the ends of the ages have come" (1 Cor. 10:11).

"For whatsoever things were written before were written for our learning, that we through the patience and of the scriptures might have hope" (Rom. 15:4). (The word hope here is elpís, meaning, to anticipate, to expect what is sure or certain. —Strong's #1680)

— *Chapter 1* —

IN THE BEGINNING, GOD!

Throughout the Bible, our Great God, by His Holy Spirit, inspired men to write many scriptural accounts of His working in the lives of His people. I see the concept or representation of fellowship characteristics throughout the Bible or Holy Scriptures, even from the very beginning before creation.

I believe it started with the only true God Himself, known and called by many YHWH (Yahweh), Adonai, Jehovah (or Yehovah), or Lord.

"In the beginning God created the heaven and the earth. And the earth was without form, and void; and darkness was upon the face of the deep. And the Spirit of God moved upon the face of the waters. Then God said, let there be light, and there was light" (Gen. 1:1–2).

"For thus says the Lord, Who created the heavens, Who is God, Who formed the earth and made it, Who has established it, Who did not create it in vain, Who formed it to be inhabited: 'I am the Lord, and there is no other'" (Isa. 45:18).

The Hebrew word used for God here is Elohim, which is plural and yet One. Only God can be as He is, Father, Son, and Holy Spirit. Many have tried to decipher God and have asked how this can be. I just believe and simply take Him at His Word, that He is who He say He is. To help me grasp this with my finite thinking, I consider the fact that I am a husband to my wife, father to my children, son to my mother, brother to my siblings, yet I am one man.

God created the earth to be inhabited by His people, representing Him, extending His kingdom's influences therein. Yes, God—Elohim—creates everything with purpose. You and I, made in His image and likeness, are part of His overall plan and desires for His earth.

Jesus the Christ, while on earth, housed the fullness of the Godhead or divine nature of God. I daily remind myself that the Godhead worked as one to bring me into salvation. God so loved me that He gave me Jesus. Jesus so loved me that He sacrificed Himself. And Holy Spirit so loved me that He convicted me of sin as he moved upon my soul with the love of God inviting me to fellowship-walk with the Elohim.

I encourage you to read and meditate on the promises of Colossians, chapter 2, and get the entire message of how this fullness of God that was in Christ completes the children of God, letting us know that no matter what we face in life we face such with the fullness of the Godhead. I have come to realize that all of whom Christ dwells or lives in by His Spirit has been spiritually positioned far above all spiritual beings, powers, and authorities in heaven and the earth.

Throughout Scripture, Jesus often commented about He and Father God being One. On one occasion, He prayed that the children of God, His church, would become one as He and God the Father are one so that the world would know that He is the only true God. This becoming one is more than a relationship; it is fellowshipping, partnering, and participating together as one people to the Glory of God. This is so needed in our day and time as the world looks on. An excellent read regarding the oneness of God in Christ is in John 17.

Chapter 2

FIRST MAN—
ADAM AND EVE

Then God said, "Let Us make man in Our image, accord-
ing to Our likeness; let them have dominion over the fish of
the sea, over the birds of the air, and over the cattle, over
all the earth and over every creeping thing that creeps on
the earth." So, God created man in His own image; in the
image of God He created him; male and female He created
them.

GENESIS 1:26–27

T he word God in this verse is also Elohim, a plural
noun. The word *Us* is also plural, informing the
readers there was more than just the one speaking
during the creation of all things (heavens, earth, and the
making of man), drawing attention to the intimate fellowship of the Almighty Elohim. Hence, fellowship, not merely
relationship.

Man was made in the image and likeness of God with fellowship in mind. Hence, man was created by One who, within and of Himself fellowshipped, and man being made in God's image and likeness was created to fellowship with Him (God) and man (each other). The person-to-person fellowship began with Adam and Eve, husband and wife. They were to populate earth with the same concept, showing forth the character and likeness of the One who created them.

There came a time after Adam and Eve were made that they sinned by disobeying God's word to them to not eat of the tree of the knowledge of good and evil. Their disobedience caused a change in their relationship. It went from fellowship (God walking with them) to relationship (them trying to hide themselves from God). Now, we know God is omnipresent, so He knew their whereabouts. He drew attention to what their sin of disobedience had caused—it affected their fellowship.

"And they heard the sound of the Lord God walking in the garden in the cool of the day, and Adam and his wife hid themselves from the presence of the Lord God among the trees of the garden. Then the Lord God called to Adam and said to him, 'Where are you?' So, he said, 'I heard Your voice in the garden, and I was afraid because I was naked; and I hid myself.' And He said, 'Who told you that you were naked? Have you eaten from the tree of which I commanded you that you should not eat?' Then the man said, 'The woman whom You gave to be with me, she gave me of the tree, and I ate" (Gen. 3:8–12).

Adam blamed Eve for their sin of disobedience. Yep, he deflected all the blame on Eve. God gave Adam the responsibility and authority to lead and protect his wife and their fellowship with one another. Instead, he separated himself from any wrongdoing and blamed Eve, his wife.

Adam and Eve's disobedience caused them to believe they needed to hide themselves from the presence of God. Disobedience, as well as any sin, affects fellowship to where the one that commits the sin sometimes feels he or she can't go into the presence of the one against whom the sin was committed. It sometimes brings shame along with it.

One Hebrew word for "presence" is paniym, meaning "face." I believe God enjoyed fellowship with Adam and Eve. Adam and Eve allowed another (Satan) to come in and negatively influence their thinking, thereby affecting their decision making. I can recall numerous times when I allowed others (I will call them my hang-out-with crew) to negatively affect my decision making, impeding the flow of fellowshipping with my wife, Jerlyn. Looking back at those times, I see how my helpmate's love was patient, kind, and enduring. Although I did not know the Lord during those times, I can now see how God sometimes caused me to reflect on those years, using those times to teach me about His love for me and my wife's unwavering love for me, even when I took running with the boys over staying home with her. What an example of God's and Jerlyn's love during a time of not fully appreciating the helper God gave me. Today, I am so grateful God saw my need for Jerlyn to be my wife, as He knew she was one I would cleave to, not merely relationally, but more importantly, partnering (another word for fellowshipping) with.

Marriage Instituted

"And the Lord God said, 'It is not good that man should be alone; I will make him a helper comparable to him.' And the Lord God caused a deep sleep to fall on Adam, and he slept; and He took one of his ribs and closed up the flesh in its place. Then the rib which the Lord God had taken from man He made into a woman, and He brought her to the man. And Adam said: This is now bone of my bones and flesh of my flesh; she shall be called woman, because she was taken out of man. Therefore, a man shall leave his father and mother and be joined to his wife, and they shall become one flesh" (Gen. 2:18, 21–24).

The words helper and helpmate carry the concept of fellowship. Some Hebrew definitions for the word fellowship are partnering, companion, comparable, and participant. All of which are important to always understand and keep in one's heart for a joyous and healthy marriage.

Husband and wife being joined, becoming one flesh, also carries the concept of fellowship. Becoming one does not mean becoming the same; the man and woman bring their individual God-given purposes to the marriage. They unite as one but remain unique in themselves, the way God made them to be. I think it's wonderful how God can take a man and women with different personalities and bring them together and cause both to give of themselves for the betterment of the union. As a husband, it's important that I love my wife, as Christ loved His church. I must give myself not only to her but, at times, for her. Giving myself to her says I offer myself to be a part of her life; giving myself for her says, I offer myself up to help her fulfil her God given purpose. This requires consistent communication with Jerlyn and with God about Jerlyn. I communicate with God so I learn what His desire for her is. There is more to a wife than just being married to her husband. That is definitely important, and so is the husband to his wife. However, each has a God-given purpose for which He fashioned them and brought them together. No wonder God said, who He has joined together, let no one separate or split apart. This statement is no way meant to bring shame or condemnation to anyone who has divorced, as your divorce could be for just reasons. So please do not read that into this statement. Some marriages end in divorce because of the lack of consistent fellowship. The relationship was there; however, what was missing and needed most was fellowship—intimacy, communication, cooperation, sharing, partnering, contributing from both.

Only know that when God joins man and woman as husband and wife, He does so for a loving purpose. Jerlyn and I have been married for forty years, and not all forty years were roses. Within those years, I have learned that Jerlyn respected me more when I showed more of my love and respect for her, particularly when I valued her input in decisions made regarding things relative to marriage (like finances).

Many Christian men like letting their wives know that Apostle Peter, in 1 Peter, the third chapter, wrote that wives must be submissive to their own husbands. I say to the men that as you love your wife, not in words only but also in actions, your wives will find it easy to submit to you. You, men, must consider that the word submit does not mean your wives should do so out of your dictating or commanding that they do so. Let your love draw your wife into fulfilling her God-instructed duties to you as her husband.

Men are not to be dictators or treat their wives harshly, rather they are to live with their wives with respect and love. There must be a "cleaving to and not letting go" from both. If the husband and wife both develop and keep this mindset, marriages will show forth the Glory of God.

To receive all of what marriage brings, there must be consistent and genuine marriage fellowship. This is vital to keeping the marriage healthy. God has given both the husband and wife His grace to carry out their roles and responsibilities within the marriage.

— Chapter 3 —

ENOCH

Enoch lived sixty-five years, and begot Methuselah. After he begot Methuselah, Enoch walked with God three hundred years, and had sons and daughters. So, all the days of Enoch were three hundred and sixty-five years. And Enoch walked with God; and he was not, for God took him.

GENESIS 5:21–24

The phrase "walked with God," shows that Enoch accompanied, kept pace with, continued along with God. Yes, Enoch continued along with God until he was taken up to heaven to be with God. Fellowship with God through Christ will cause one to continue to walk with Him and not lose heart, even when times during the walk become tough and trying. When my wife and I got the word of our son's passing, we knew the only way through that tough time was through "fellowship with God and with each other," walking with God and walking with each other, being each other's support. In fellowship-walking with God, you will always know He is there, for He said He will never leave nor forsake you. In relationship-walking, you could give way to thoughts that He is not with you, that you are alone. Not so, says fellowship-walking with God. This will cause you to see yourself being taken up into the glorious and caring arms of the Lord.

It is written of Enoch that before God took him; he had a testimony that he pleased God. No, it was not of the sort where a person during church services stands up and tells of all the things the Lord has given and done for the person. I believe in doing this when given the opportunity to do so, as I enjoy publicly thanking our Lord for all He has done for me, and hearing what He has done and is doing in the lives of others is encouraging. Isaiah 26:12 states, "Lord, you establish peace for us; all that we have accomplished You have done for us." I remind myself of this scripture daily as I know my accomplishments are because of His Grace working in and through my life.

Back to Enoch's testimony. His testimony was that he pleased God. There's not a word about what God did for him or gave him. I'm sure Enoch appreciated all God did for him. Using my imagination, I see Enoch just walking with God, and the fellowship is so good to both Enoch and God that God says to Enoch, "Come with Me, son. I am bringing you to an even better place of fellowship with Me—the place prepared for you from the beginning of time. I want it to be said of me, before I leave this side of heaven to be with the Lord, that my testimony was such that it pleased God. I not only want to hear God say, "well done, my good a faithful servant,"

I want Him to say, "Johnnie, your entire walk after coming to know Me, pleased Me. You obeyed and done all I asked of you." I imagine this is the testimony Enoch had too—that by faith, he obeyed all that was asked of him by God. Faith was key to Enoch's walk, and faith is key to my and your walk with God. I can only please God by my faith in Him and my obedience to His word to me. (A wonderful read about Enoch and others being commended for their faith in God can be found in Hebrews 11).

— *Chapter 4* —

NOAH

By faith Noah, being divinely warned of things not yet seen, moved with godly fear (or reverence), prepared an ark for the saving of his household, by which he condemned the world and became heir of the righteousness which is according to faith."

HEBREWS 11:7

G od said, and Noah did. During Noah's life, people indulged in much wickedness, like what we see on the earth today, so much so that God was sorry He had made man on the earth. You know things had to be bad for it to grieve God that He said this. God even said, "I will destroy man whom I have created from the face of the earth, both man and beast, creeping thing and birds of the air, for I am sorry that I have made them" (Gen. 6:7).

But Noah's character and behavior differed from that of the others, so much so that it was said that "Noah found grace in the eyes of the Lord" (Gen. 6:8b).

What about Noah's life led God to look at him and see grace in him? For starters, Noah walked with God, indicating he had fellowship with the Almighty. But I see two wonderful characteristics of Noah's walk with the Lord in Genesis 6:9, where it is written, "This is the genealogy of Noah.

Noah was a just man, perfect in his generations. Noah walked with God." Noah was a just man, righteous in his character and actions. And he was perfect, having integrity, sound judgement of his surroundings, and undefiled by the unrighteous activities of those in his generations. I believe Noah showed faith and obedience, no matter how silly the acts of his obedience were to the people in his day. Consider being asked by God to build an ark, something you have never heard of or seen before. Consider the stares and gossip of the people in his day while he was building something, they too had never seen or heard of. Nevertheless, Noah obeyed his God. I see trust in Noah, from God to him, and from him to and in God. The kind of trust that's built through consistent fellowship with one another. How about Noah's sons? They, too, had to have seen the faces and heard the words their father heard while they built the ark. Nevertheless, Noah did as God commanded him. What wonderful examples of fellowship with God by Noah and of father–son fellowship between Noah and his sons. God said, and Noah did. I imagine his sons believed and trusted in their father as he led the family, believing and trusting solely in his God. I believe Noah's sons' wives trusted and believed in their husbands, for they, too, must have heard the gossip and seen the stares of the people. I imagine the people around them saying something like, "Noah and his sons done lost their minds. They done gone too far this time, talking about some major rainstorm is coming. Yeah, right!" However, at the word of his God, he obeyed. I imagine Noah thinking, "There must be a whole lot of rain (water) coming, as per the measurements and all the animals and things I must bring inside it, this is going to be a very large boat once finished."

Fellowship-walking with God will cause your obedience, at times, to appear foolish to those looking at it from the outside, but know that obeying God brings blessings—blessings in what He rewards you with and, more importantly, the blessing of knowing Him and knowing you have done what pleases Him. One thing I know for sure is that obeying Him pleases Him and gives Him joy. It's a beautiful thing to live in a way that brings God joy. It is His joy that gives me strength.

When God instructed Noah to come out of the ark after the flood, Noah was told that he, his sons, and their wives were to be fruitful and multiply. This brings to mind the words spoken to Adam and Eve: "Be fruitful and multiply and have dominion." (Gen. 1:28) God's desire and purpose have not changed. He wants man to populate the earth with His likeness, having dominion and authority.

My desire is to get to a point in my fellowship with God at which no matter what He commands or asks of me, I do it with no hesitation. I believe we can all get to that place in our walk with Him that God says of us that we are not only just and perfect through the blood of Christ Jesus, but we are walking and living as such in the earth, our communities, and our cities. In Christ, this is available and possible for everyone that receives Him as Savior and Lord. Christ is our Living Redeemer, Halleluiah!

--- *Chapter 5* ---

ABRAM (ABRAHAM)

And when Abram was ninety years old and nine, the Lord appeared to Abram, and said unto him, I am the Almighty God; walk before me, and be thou perfect. And I will make my covenant between me and thee and will multiply thee exceedingly. And Abram fell on his face: and God talked with him, saying, as for me, behold, my covenant is with thee, and thou shalt be a father of many nations. Neither shall thy name any more be called Abram, but thy name shall be Abraham; for a father of many nations have I made thee.

GENESIS 17:1–5

By faith Abraham obeyed when he was called to go out to the place which he would receive as an inheritance. And he went out, not knowing where he was going.

HEBREWS 11:8–10

A person is never too old (or young) to be called by God for a purpose that only God has in mind. Abram was ninety-nine years of age when he was called by God to be the father (father here denotes "fellowship," as a father affects the lives of his children). God, from the very beginning, created man to affect each other's lives, like he affects ours, with love, mercy, kindness, and grace. I imagine when God looks at a man like He did Abraham, He sees some of Himself in that man. One of the noble qualities of Abraham was his faith, which lead to his obedience, which was accounted to him as righteousness, and Abraham is one of the Hall of Faith Memorial listed in Hebrews 11.

God asked Abraham to walk before Him, and in doing so, God would multiply Abraham's seed exceedingly. This is interesting, as with Adam and Eve, and with Noah, God told them to multiply, but here God tells Abraham, He would multiply him. Yes, God said He would cause Abraham to multiply and be a father of many nations (ethnicities or ethnic groups). This multiplicity was contingent upon Abraham's obedience to walk before God, hence a place of fellowship with God.

Abraham's obedience, by faith to God's word, brought "covenant fellowship," full of promises and a name change.

When God called to Abraham, Abraham fell on his face. Falling on his face symbolizes humility. This is a wonderful character to have. I'm not talking about a false sense of humility, but genuine humility where it's God or nothing. It's honoring God before all people and all things. When you honor God, He will cause you to honor others, and doing so will be without reservation. I realize that sometimes I can hear clearer when I am prostrated or laying before God, not just in posture but more importantly, prostrated in heart, mind, soul, and spirit—all of me. I can't explain why that is. All I know is that sometimes it is that way. I can also hear the Lord while sitting or in the standing position. I am just saying there is something about falling on my face before His presence. Consistent fellowship makes this a consistent response to His manifested presence.

Abraham's consistent fellowship with God, I believe, is directly reflected in God's conversation about him when God said, while discussing what He had planned to do about the sinful activities in Sodom, "Shall I hide from Abraham what I am doing, since Abraham shall surely become a great and mighty nation, and all the nations of the earth shall be blessed in him? For I have known him, in order that he may command his children and his household after him, that they keep the way of the Lord, to do righteousness and justice, that the Lord may bring to Abraham what He has spoken to him" (Gen. 18:17–18). (See the entire chapter of Genesis 18 for the complete story.)

The word *known* indicates intimacy or fellowship. Abraham's time of fellowship with God benefitted Lot and his family, as Lot and his family were living in Sodom. Our consistent fellowship with God can benefit others in our families and those we associate with either through friendships or work relations. There have been numerous times because of my relationship with family, friends, and coworkers that I have learned of prayer needs and acted accordingly interceded on their behalf. I'm sure others have done the same for me and my family. Fellowshipping with God places us in position to hear of the needs of others, and it gives us opportunities to act as Abraham did for his nephew Lot and others in Sodom.

Fellowship between God and Abraham was of such to where God let Abraham know what His plans were regarding Sodom. After God let Abraham in on the plan, Abraham went into his fathering mode or instinct and interceded for Sodom. I am of the belief that Abraham was not ignorant of the activities within Sodom; he knew of the lawlessness and sinfulness of the folks in Sodom.

Abraham obeyed God and left the environment he was familiar with, not knowing anything about the place or land he was going to. He had only the word of God, and that was enough for him. I have learned during my life with God, that consistent fellowship with Him by His Holy Spirit has caused me to trust in Him beyond my understanding.

For Abraham to move at this word, he must have had a relationship that moved into one of fellowship. As Holy Spirit has encouraged me to consistently walk before Him in fellowship, I have thought that perhaps Abraham had relationship with God, and when God called him to leave some of his family, friends, and the environment he lived in, the moment Abraham trusted and obeyed God's word to him, that was the moment his walk and knowledge of God changed from a mere relationship one to fellowship.

Abraham's fellowship-faith and fellowship-obedience to God, I believe, contributed to Abraham's enemies being placed in his hands, defeated, and caused others to bless him. Likewise, fellowship with God by His Holy Spirit will cause others to bless you and say of you, "You are blessed of the Lord, because of the hand of God upon you."

— *Chapter 6* —

JOB

There was a man in the land of Uz, whose name was Job; and that man was blameless and upright, and one who feared God and shunned evil.

Then the Lord said to Satan, "Have you considered My servant Job, that there is none like him on the earth, a blameless and upright man, one who fears God and shuns evil?" So, Satan answered the Lord and said, "Does Job fear God for nothing? Have You not made a hedge around him, around his household, and around all that he has on every side? You have blessed the work of his hands, and his possessions have increased in the land. But now, stretch out Your hand and touch all that he has, and he will surely curse You to Your face!

JOB 1:1 AND 8–11

S atan noticed the hedge or fence of protection around Job. Satan must have been trying to get at Job, but recognized Job had something going for him that others during his time did not; he had great reverence for God, and he was "upright," meaning Job was a meek and humbled man, and this pleased God to where God knew more of Job than Job and Satan knew of Job. God knew His servant Job would not draw back from believing and trusting in Him. (That he "knew" him shows intimacy or fellowship.) A man or woman of God that has gone from relationship to fellowship with God has a presence about him or her that the enemy recognizes. Now, I do not advocate for anyone to ask the Lord to have Satan try him as he tried Job, but what a testimony of Job to where God, Creator of heaven and earth and all that are within it, to have such confidence and faith in Job that he would not deny Him, no matter the persecution. One of the Hebrew meanings for the name Job is "persecution." How would you like to have a name that means persecution? I do not know if Job knew what his name meant—I assume he did, since that was the norm during that time, to know what names meant, yet he revered God to the end, even if it meant him perishing. Job had a tough series of life-changing moments: his sons and daughters were killed by a very strong wind, he had material possessions destroyed (he was a wealthy man), and he was stricken in his body with sickness and disease, yet Job did not speak ill about or toward his God. Rather, Job, during all those trials and devastating circumstances, worshipped God. This attitude or character comes at a place of fellowship, not merely relational.

Considering the concept of fellowship, for Satan to say, "Job will curse God to His face," shows Job had spent some face-to-face time with God. How this was done I don't know, but what I do know is that it was done, otherwise Job would not have had the strength and faith to hold on to his God during the trials he endured. Even Job's wife wanted him to give up and curse God and just die. Wow, now that was some helpmate—not! Obviously, Job's wife did not walk with God as Job did. Perhaps she enjoyed the hand of God, the things God gave Job and his family, and not God Himself. Job's response to all the things he endured shows a man that had great intimacy and trust with and in God. To develop such faith, trust, and reliance, one must position oneself through fellowship with God.

I remember when my wife, Jerlyn, and I got the news of the passing of our son, who was twenty-nine years of age at his passing, how painful that news was, as I had many of times envisioned our son and I walking, fellowshipping together as we both lived out the purpose of God for our lives. I was confused. Many thoughts ran through my mind, even thoughts like, "Does this God I trust really care about me and my family?" Yes, as a man that truly loves the Lord, I had a moment of questioning all of this and God. However, leaning on God and in God through fellowship with Him through His Spirit, and declaring His word over me and my wife, Jerlyn, a few days after receiving that news of his passing and days of laying and crying out before Father God, and while on my knees, I heard God say so plainly, "I know you and Jerlyn are hurting. Do you want me to take this pain and hurt away today, tomorrow, next week, or next month?" I responded, Lord, please take this hurt and confusion away now. I tell you: it was instant! From that moment onward, I was free and was comfortable talking about my son's passing to anyone without the hurt I felt after receiving the news of his passing. I can't say that I know what Job felt during his many trials. What I can say and am saying, is God has proven to me that the more I fellowship with Him, the things I face in this life His Spirit makes all the difference in the world with my getting through it all. There is truly a peace in God that will pass one's understanding. There also came a strength beyond my understanding, and there is a comfort from the Comforter, His Holy Spirit. You may have experienced similar trials as me and Jerlyn. I ask you to allow the peace, strength, comfort, and love of God to saturate your being. There is where He is and will always be. Let God take the hurt, pain, and confusion from you today, in Jesus' Name!

"I have heard of You by the hearing of the ear, but now my eye sees You. Therefore, I abhor myself, and repent in dust and ashes. And so it was, after the Lord had spoken these words to Job, that the Lord said to Eliphaz the Temanite, 'My wrath is aroused against you and your two friends, for you have not spoken of Me what is right, as My servant Job has. Now therefore, take for yourselves seven bulls and seven rams, go to My servant Job, and offer up for yourselves a burnt offering; and My servant Job shall pray for you. For I will accept him, lest I deal with you according to your folly; because you have not spoken of Me what is right, as My servant Job has.' So Eliphaz the Temanite and Bildad the Shuhite and Zophar the Naamathite went and did as the Lord commanded them; for the Lord had accepted Job. And the Lord restored Job's losses when he prayed for his friends.

Indeed, the Lord gave Job twice as much as he had before"
(Job 42:5–10).

Job's statement, "I heard of You but now my eyes see You,"
shows a relationship (Job hearing of God) that moved to fellowship (now I know You). God's communication with Job
pointed out to Job, and me, that consistent conversing with,
walking with, fellowshipping with God will cause a child of
God to go from "I heard about You" to "I know You Lord."
When I became born again, in the first few years of being a
child of God, I heard much about Jesus. Now, after years of
walking with Jesus, I can confidently say, "I know Him."

The Lord accepted Job and used him as a go between for
Eliphaz and his friends. It was Job who God chose for them to
take their sacrifices to, to atone for their misrepresentation of
God. Fellowship with God has caused me on many occasions
to stand in prayer for those who have talked wrongly about
me, for those who had falsely accused me of doing or saying
something I did not do or say. This position has helped keep
my mind on God no matter the difficulties faced. I remember
having to minister healing to someone during the same time
I needed healing from hearing the news regarding my son.
Only a healing God can do that, and He did for me. I rested in
that place of fellowship with God and by His grace imparted
to the person on the other end of the phone on that day what
that person needed, yes, even during a time of my need. Halleluiah!

— *Chapter 7* —

MOSES

And the child grew, and she brought him to Pharaoh's daughter, and he became her son. So, she called his name Moses, saying, "Because I drew him out of the water.

EXODUS 2:10

I am the God of your father, the God of Abraham, the God of Isaac, and the God of Jacob." And Moses hid his face, for he was afraid to look upon God. And the Lord said: "I have surely seen the oppression of My people who are in Egypt, and have heard their cry because of their taskmasters, for I know their sorrows. So, I have come down to deliver them out of the hand of the Egyptians, and to bring them up from that land to a good and large land, to a land flowing with milk and honey.

EXODUS 3:6–8

So, the Lord spoke to Moses face to face, as a man speaks to his friend.

EXODUS 33:11

Although Pharaoh's daughter had Moses fetched out of the pond, his birth mother was the one who actually nurtured him, unbeknown to Pharaoh's daughter. What age he was when taken to Pharaoh's daughter, I can only guess. Scripture documents that Moses grew, and then he was taken to Pharaoh's daughter to become her son. I imagine, while being reared as a little child, those nursing him shared with Moses their faith and teachings. This, I believe, was foundational to Moses' responses to God later in life. I was also in a pond when God fetched me out and named me one of His own. Since then, all I have done and do are in relation to that moment of Him drawing me out of my sin into His righteousness.

At the time of being pulled out of the pond, none of Moses' family or those in Pharoah's house had any thoughts the Hand of God would later use Moses as God's chosen man (vessel) to pull the children of Israel out of their pond of bondage of the Egyptians. This reminds me of an email I received several years ago from a very good friend of me and my wife to let me know of her thankfulness of our God, using my wife and I as tools in His hands to draw her, and later her husband, out of their pond of bondage so to speak. My commentating of the email conversation relative to this train of thought shows and encourages me of how my wife and I through fellowshipping with God (although we were thinking relationship at that time) was used to bring others into His Kingdom by His Son, Jesus.

I love the concept of fellowship I see when God called to Moses from the bush that burned but was not consumed.

God, to Moses, said, "I am the God of your father." To me, father has always been, and will always be, more than a relationship, as it means so much more after living my entire life without my father, not because he was not alive during my life, but because he was not willing to be such to me, in my life. But God will be a Father to the fatherless. He was for me and continues to be. I can see how I was under oppression, by a different type of pharaoh and Egypt. For me, it was the oppression of a sinful life without Christ. I now live a life flowing with spiritual milk and honey, a life in God through Christ Jesus. Hence, fellowshipping with Christ through the person of His Spirit.

During the clouds by day and the fire by night, as God lead the children of Israel through the wilderness, they grew comfortable with God as their God, and they, His people "relationship," but preferred Moses go up and talk with, fellowship with God on behalf of them and bring the laws to them. It was Moses that enjoyed God allowing him to have face to face with Him. The word *face* here in Hebrew is paniym. This same word is sometimes translated as presence, as the part that turns.

Moses' fellowship with God was also covenant. God said, God promised, Moses heard, and Moses did. Through Moses, God told the children of Israel that He would be their God and they His people. Only, abide by My laws. God does not need people to be complete. I believe, He wanted a people to experience His love, as a father and mother their children.

Fellowshipping with God allows Him to write His laws in my heart, so that I do not sin against Him or man.

God chose to deliver His people by Moses. Moses would fulfil this deliverance of God's people by fellowship-walking with God, doing all of what He said to do. God even buried Moses Himself rather than let someone else do it. You can read about this and the many signs and wonders done by God through Moses in Deuteronomy 34.

Moses's fellowship with God leaves an example of communication between our Great God and His chosen servant and this servant's heart toward His God and the people of His God.

— *Chapter 8* —

JOSHUA AND CALEB

Then they told him and said: "We went to the land where you sent us. It truly flows with milk and honey, and this is its fruit. Nevertheless, the people who dwell in the land are strong; the cities are fortified and very large; moreover, we saw the descendants of Anak there. Then Caleb quieted the people before Moses, and said, "Let us go up at once and take possession, for we are well able to overcome it. But the men who had gone up with him said, "We are not able to go up against the people, for they are stronger than we. And they gave the children of Israel a bad report of the land which they had spied out, saying, "The land through which we have gone as spies is a land that devours its inhabitants, and all the people whom we saw in it are men of great stature. There we saw the giants (the descendants of Anak came from the giants); and we were like grasshoppers in our own sight, and so we were in their sight.

NUMBERS 13:27–33

Surely none of the men who came up from Egypt, from twenty years old and above, shall see the land of which I swore to Abraham, Isaac, and Jacob, because they have not wholly followed Me, except Caleb the son of Jephunneh, the Kenizzite, and Joshua the son of Nun, for they have wholly followed the Lord.

NUMBERS 32:11–12

J oshua and Caleb's minds were set on the word spoken by their God by the mouth and actions of their God appointed leader, Moses. The other ten spies' minds were set on what they saw in the land (giants, fortified cities) and themselves. The other ten saw defeat. Joshua and Caleb were convinced Moses heard from God to possess the land, so through their eyes they saw victory. All twelve men had the same background: bondage in Egypt, Passover, Red Sea Crossing, had seen God supply their needs time after time again. But what was seen of God resonated deep within the spirits and souls of only two of the spies, Joshua and Caleb. How we walk in our day largely depends on what we resonate with, how we see God, and how we see ourselves in our own eyes, conquered or conquerors, victims or victorious. Joshua and Caleb saw their God greater and above the inhabitants of the land and their fortified walls. These two men had a we-can-do-it, we-are-more-than-able mindset with God leading them. I believe this mindset was due to Joshua and Caleb meditating on the words they received from the mouth of Moses as though it was directly from God Himself to them directly. They trusted the man of God. Therefore, when they heard the words spoken by Moses the words took on a different meaning than the others hearing the same words. I am not advocating following a man or woman of God blindly. Try the spirit of the person and if you know God has placed a particular person and ministry in your life to help lead and guide you to fulfilling God's plan and purpose for your life, then trust God and trust that person until Holy Spirit show you otherwise.

"Now Joshua the son of Nun was full of the spirit of wisdom, for Moses had laid his hands on him; so, the children of Israel heeded him, and did as the Lord had commanded Moses" (Deut. 34:9–10).

I envision Joshua walked with Moses as Moses walked with God, and that fellowship he had with Moses put him in position to receive of a like anointing, as Joshua learned at the feet of Moses. Joshua's fellowship with Moses helped in his fellowship and trust in the God of Moses, who was also Joshua's God. Joshua had to know God for himself.

This same attitude Joshua had went with him on the battlefield, where he knew victory was always in the hands of his God. Joshua often showed no hesitation when instructed by Moses to choose men to lead into battle against Israel's enemies. Fellowship-walking with the Spirit of God will cause you to see what others can't or do not care to see. And, it will cause you to see victory over the enemies in the land you have been sent to possess and occupy.

This is another reason why I think a mere relationship with God will not do it. Fellowshipping with Him is where it's at!

The other ten men sent to spy out the land probably prayed relationally based on what they thought they knew about God, but failed to enter the place of prayer where Joshua and Caleb entered. Joshua and Caleb prayed with the mindset of "knowing" God and not just knowing about Him. Fellowship will take you there.

After the death of Moses, God told Joshua to move out, lead the people of Israel to the land promised them, and that every place Joshua's foot would tread had already been given him. Get this—God, who knows all things, who knows the end from the beginning, said to Joshua, where you go, I have already given it to you, before you reach that place, Joshua, I have already prepared it for your taking.

It seems the only thing God required of Joshua was; be strong and courageous, observe to do according to all the laws given to them by God, and to meditate in the Law. Doing so would make them prosperous and have good success, for God promised He would be with Joshua. (I see this in Joshua 1.)

Who has God called you to lead and help get to where they need to get to? Enter a place of fellowship with Him and allow His Spirit to guide you.

— *Chapter 9* —

SAMUEL

Samuel, as a little boy, was taken by his mother, Hannah, to Eli the prophet, where he was mentored and groomed for the Lord. Eli and Samuel had such a relationship that Samuel often called Eli "father" and Eli often called Samuel "son." For Eli to feel comfortable calling another person's child his son, he must have developed a fellowship relationship with Samuel. (See 1 Samuel 2 and 3.)

Samuel was recognized as a man of God in whatever city he went. I believe this was because of his fellowship with God.

"Now the donkeys of Kish, Saul's father, were lost. And Kish said to his son Saul, please take one of the servants with you, and arise, go and look for the donkeys. When they had come to the land of Zuph, Saul said to his servant who was with him, 'Come, let us return, lest my father cease caring about the donkeys and become worried about us.' And he said to him, 'Look now, there is in this city a man of God, and he is an honorable man; all that he says surely comes to pass.

So, let us go there; perhaps he can show us the way that we should go.

"So, they went up to the city. As they were coming into the city, there was Samuel, coming out toward them on his way up to the high place. Now the Lord had told Samuel in his ear the day before Saul came, saying, 'Tomorrow about this time I will send you a man from the land of Benjamin, and you shall anoint him commander over My people Israel, that he may save My people from the hand of the Philistines; for I have looked upon My people, because their cry has come to Me.' So, when Samuel saw Saul, the Lord said to him, "There he is, the man of whom I spoke to you. This one shall reign over My people"" (1 Sam. 9:3, 5–6, 14–17).

It was Saul's servant that informed Saul that he had heard of Samuel, and that Samuel was in the city they had come to in search for the lost donkeys. I think for Saul to choose this servant out of the others, and to heed the advice of his servant, Saul and this servant must have had a good relationship that probably grew into one of fellowship to where Saul had developed a trust in this servant and welcomed and valued this servant's suggestion to go see Samuel. Fellowship tends to lead to trusting in another to help you find what you are looking for, and to come to know what is missing in your walk with the Lord. I can contest to this as fellowship with Holy Spirit has helped me come to know my reason for being.

Saul's servant had heard that Samuel was an honorable man. This is a reputation worth noting. Honorable people are known for fairness, being trustworthy, loving and having and showing genuine respect toward all people, no matter their nationality or skin color.

The more children of God fellowship with Holy Spirit, the more they will know how to honor and represent God in the places they live.

God spoke to Samuel in his ear. Now, that isn't odd in itself, since we hear with our ears. But it says a lot about Samuel and God's intimacy. To speak in someone's ear, you must get in close. Samuel had such intimacy with God, so much so that when something grieved God, it grieved him. It is recorded in 1 Samuel 15, that God said to Samuel that it repented Him that He anointed Saul as king. This was after Saul disobeyed the word of the Lord to destroy his enemies and all their possessions. Saul however, decided not to do so and instead kept some of the possessions. The reason I point this out is not to focus on Saul's disobedience, but to draw focus to the prophet Samuel's response. It grieved Samuel when he heard of King Saul's disobedience, to where Samuel cried before God all that night. Here is a man so intimate with God, to where what touch God, touched him, to where what grieved God, grieved him. I had an experience along this thinking I share in the section on dreams, the one about the old-style mob head.

Chapter 10

DAVID AND JONATHAN

Now Saul spoke to Jonathan his son and to all his servants, that they should kill David; but Jonathan, Saul's son, delighted greatly in David. So, Jonathan told David, saying, "My father Saul seeks to kill you. Therefore, please be on your guard until morning, and stay in a secret place and hide.

1 SAMUEL 19:1–2

Now Jonathan again caused David to vow, because he loved him; for he loved him as he loved his own soul.

1 SAMUEL 20:17

King Saul's son, Jonathan, had a close relationship with David, which I believe blossomed because of their fellowship with one another. Their souls were knitted together. There was a time when David knew Saul had become jealous of him, as the people would sing songs of Saul slaying his thousands, and David his tens of thousands.

Saul's jealously led to him wanting David killed. David had learned of this and told it to Jonathan. At first, Jonathan didn't believe his dad would want David killed. When Jonathan learned David was right about this, Jonathan was grieved because of the shame his father Saul had brought upon him. Therefore, Jonathan encouraged David to get away from the threat of his father. I believe Jonathan's actions resulted from his close friendship and fellowship with David. Jonathan went against his father's desire to have David killed. Instead, he warned David of his father's plans.

I have close friends that I fellowship with that I know would not hesitate to be there for me and my family should we ever need them, and they know that I would be there for them. Through our fellowship we have become family.

God chose and anointed David as king to replace Saul. God saw David as a man after His own heart, as David sought to honor and please God. I know David as king had his issues. He had Uriah placed on the first line of battle so he would be killed by the enemy soldiers during the battle, so David could have Bathsheba as his own wife, knowing she was pregnant with David's child. I mention this to show that David's shortcomings did not keep him from pursuing the heart of God. Nor did David's sin keep God from using him. Why? Because David knew how to humble himself and truly repent from his sins as captured in 2 Samuel 12, where, when the Prophet Nathan spoke to him of his sins regarding Uriah and Bathsheba, David humbled himself, repented, and cried out for forgiveness.

Consistent fellowship with God positions a person to receive conviction of sins by Holy Spirit and will cause immediate repentance.

Chapter II

ELIJAH

And he stretched himself out on the child three times, and cried out to the Lord and said, "O Lord my God, I pray, let this child's soul come back to him." Then the Lord heard the voice of Elijah; and the soul of the child came back to him, and he revived. And Elijah took the child and brought him down from the upper room into the house and gave him to his mother. And Elijah said, "See, your son lives! Then the woman said to Elijah, "Now by this I know that you are a man of God, and that the word of the Lord in your mouth is the truth.

1 KINGS 17:21–24

Then it happened, as they continued on and talked, that suddenly a chariot of fire appeared with horses of fire and separated the two of them; and Elijah went up by a whirlwind into heaven.

2 KINGS 2:11

Elijah's fellowship with God is evident throughout the books of 1 and 2 Kings. I will point out here what I will call "power-display of fellowship." So powerful that God moved at Elijah's request to restore the woman's son back to life. So powerful that God anointed Elijah to speak as He speaks. When Elijah asked Elisha, what did he want from him, and Elisha replied that he wanted a double portion of the anointing that was on Elijah. This is a powerful display of what is possible when a man or woman develop intimacy with God. Elijah didn't pray to God. Instead, he spoke the blessing upon Elisha. I believe he somehow knew God would be fine with him declaring a double portion anointing upon Elisha. This is walking with God at a level where a person is so into God, and God into that person, that the person knows without praying what God is fine with, and not okay with. I see fellowship with God bringing His people to that place in Him. The place of knowing when and what to say without asking God. Fellowship with and in Holy Spirit will get us there.

I imagine Elisha took notice that Elijah walked and operated as one having access to a power and authority from a place other than earth. Elijah walked as one having access to the Kingdom of God. I contributed this to his fellowship with God.

I believe we are in times (with pandemic, racial injustice, and unrest) where God will use those that fellowship-walk with His Spirit like He used Elijah to draw people to His love and mercy. On one account, Elijah prayed earnestly that it would not rain; and it did not rain on the land for three years and six months. (Refer to James 5, and 1 Kings 17 and 18.)

— *Chapter 12* —

GOD SO LOVED
THE WORLD

For God so loved the world that He gave His only begotten Son, that whoever believes in Him should not perish but have everlasting life.

JOHN 3:16

God's love showed in a manner beyond human comprehension. First off, He gave Himself for the entire world, not just man. I believe the "whoever" applies to man, but Christ went to the cross to restore all things affected by one man's sin of disobedience. What a wonderful display of love, where God took on flesh and the cross for me, for you. There is no fellowship with God without the cross! For, without the shedding of blood there is no remission of sin, nor a means to enter into fellowship with God. Those that come to Him must believe that He is who He say He is, and that He is a rewarded for those that seek Him with all their hearts. The reward is beyond things, although He gives us things. The reward is Himself, giving those that receives Him the opportunity to know Him through fellowshipping with Him by His Spirit and reading and meditating in His Word. Yes, God so loved the world that He sent His only begotten son to bring us into fellowship with Him, the fellowship the first Adam had. Halleluiah!

God is a loving and faithful God. He is reliable, trustworthy, and dependable. By Him I was called into companionship and participation with His Son, Christ Jesus my Lord.

"That which was from the beginning, which we have heard, which we have seen with our eyes, which we have looked upon, and our hands have handled, concerning the Word of life, the life was manifested, and we have seen, and bear witness, and declare to you that eternal life which was with the Father and was manifested to us, that which we have seen and heard we declare to you, that you also may have fellowship with us; and truly our fellowship is with the Father and with His Son Jesus Christ. And these things we write to you that your joy may be full" (1 John 1–4).

Fellowship with God brings joy in its fullness. Apostle John says, "This is the message he heard from Jesus; have fellowship with Christ and one another. Consistent fellowship with Him helps keep my walking with and fellowshipping with other brothers and sisters in the spirit of Christ, shining His light through me for others to see, and be drawn to it.

Being born-again put me in relationship with Father through Christ Jesus. Fellowship with Christ by His Spirit enables me to fulfill His purpose for my being created.

Christ has purpose for me and you. Once a person comes to Christ, He imparts His power in him or her to become a son or daughter of God. That is great news, that Christ gives to the person who comes to, and accepts Him, the grace and encouragement to desire intimacy with Him.

—— *Chapter 13* ——

PRODIGAL SON

A certain man had two sons. And the younger of them said to his father, father, give me the portion of goods that falls to me. So, he divided to them his livelihood. And not many days after, the younger son gathered all together, journeyed to a far country, and there wasted his possessions with prodigal living. But when he had spent all, there arose a severe famine in that land, and he began to be in want. Then he went and joined himself to a citizen of that country, and he sent him into his fields to feed swine. And he would gladly have filled his stomach with the pods that the swine ate, and no one gave him anything. But when he came to himself, he said, "how many of my father's hired servants have bread enough and to spare, and I perish with hunger! I will arise and go to my father, and will say to him, 'father, I have sinned against heaven and before you, and I am no longer worthy to be called your son. Make me like one of your hired servants.'" And he arose and came to his father. But when he was still a great way off, his father saw him and had compassion, and ran and fell on his neck and kissed him. And the son said to him, "father, I have sinned against heaven and in your sight, and am no longer worthy to be called your son. But the father said to his servants, bring out the best robe and put it on him, and put a ring on his hand and sandals on his feet. And bring the fatted calf here and kill it and let us eat and be merry; for this my son was dead and is alive again; he was lost and is found." And they began to be merry.

LUKE 15:11–24

There are several things in these scriptures where I see the beauty of fellowship, when it is thriving, as well as when it has been taken for granted and become broken. Here are some things to consider:

The love of a father toward his son regardless of the son's rebellious actions is a lesson for any parent with a child that leaves under wrong intentions and circumstances.

Shows a father honoring a son's request, allowing him to learn from life itself, knowing the son leaving was not the best thing for him to do.

Broken fellowship could cost one to live a wasteful life, a life lower than what could have been.

Broken fellowship could open a door to famine in one's life—a life without the support needed if the fellowship was in place.

When the son was with his father, the son did not lack for any needs.

The son recalled he had a father "relationship" that he had lost fellowship with. So, the son humbled himself and got back to his father and ask for forgiveness. I imagine that act of humility and repentance brought joy to the heart of the father and started a wonderful road of fellowship again.

Repentance is key to mending any relationship to move that relationship into one of fellowship.

Father-son relationships must enter fellowship for the bond to become and remain strong. Right there is where both the father and son will receive strength.

The prodigal son and his father both missed their fellowship. I remember when my son left to go overseas to Japan, how I longed for fellowship with him. We exchange a few emails; however, the emails were more in keeping with a relationship, like, "Hi, Dad." "Hi, Son." What I longed for, and what he and I both needed, was fellowship. I write this hoping it will help someone that might read this book. Do not waste valuable time trying to figure out who was wrong or right in causing a fellowship to not become as strong as you would like between you and a loved one. Make every effort to do your part in taking the relationship into a viable fellowship, enjoying each other's presence and what each brings to the fellowship. I love where God says "Behold, I will send Elijah the prophet before the coming of the great and dreadful day of the Lord, and he will turn the hearts of the fathers to the children and the hearts of the children to their fathers". (Mal 4:5–6) What a powerful expression of God's love and desire for fathers and children—to fellowship with each other.

As with the father's eldest son, the one that did not leave home but stayed and helped his father work the family business, it appears, even though he and his father saw each other daily, perhaps they both failed to build on their relationship to where the fellowship thrived. I think this because of the comments the son made to his father when the son heard of his younger brother coming back home, and his father throwing a party to celebrate his return. It seems the eldest son got into his feelings with jealousy and told his father how he really felt about it. At a time to rejoice as a family for the return of a prodigal, he got in his feelings. Perhaps the father did not do a good enough job of letting him know that what he, the father had was always available to him, and that, if a party the elder son wanted, one could have been had at any time during their time. Or perhaps both the father and son could have done a better job at assuring each other of their worth and blessings to the other. Consistent and genuine fellowship would have helped in accomplishing this.

— *Chapter 14* —

PRAYER

I believe prayer to be at the heart of fellowship. Jesus, to his disciples, said, men always ought to pray and not lose heart (Luke 18:1).

By prayer, we communicate with Father God. Jesus, when asked by His disciples to teach them to pray, He starts by instructing them to start with "Our Father." This has fellowship all over it, for God is Abba Father. Before I can ask for His kingdom to come on earth as it is in heaven, I must start with fellowshipping with God as my Father. Jumping to kingdom come without fellowshipping with Father will not bring kingdom manifestation on our earth in the ways needed to effectively affect our cities. (For more on this, see the chapter on communities.)

Going from relationship to fellowship changed my prayers from focusing on my needs to focusing on my Master and Lord, Jesus' heart, wanting to know what pleases Him. Fellowshipping with Father causes me to love and adore Him for who He is, not for what He gives me. When I used to walk "relationship minded," my approach to God and focus was more about reminding God of what He promised me. You may ask here, are we not to remind God of His promises? Are we not to declare and confess His promises to us? Please hear me. I am not against declaring the promises of the Lord. What I am saying is, when I began to fellowship with God, my prayer focus changed to "not my will but Your (His) will be done." Fellowship with Him has caused my thoughts to be "His kingdom come, and His will be done on earth as in heaven." To me, it's not about wanting God's hand (the things He can give me). It's about desiring and knowing God's heart, what His desires are. Consider this: desiring and seeking God's heart often opens His hands to release what "He" wants a person to have for His glory! Yes, to me, it's all about God (YHVH) being glorified in and through me. In the book of Matthew, we are told to "seek first" the kingdom of God and His righteousness, and the things our King Jesus knows we have need of will be added—added because we seek Him, not seek after the things. (Read about in Matthew 6).

"Now Peter and John went up together to the temple at the hour of prayer, the ninth hour. And a certain man lame from his mother's womb was carried, whom they laid daily at the gate of the temple which is called Beautiful, to ask alms from those who entered the temple; who, seeing Peter and John about to go into the temple, asked for alms. And fixing his eyes on him, with John, Peter said, 'Look at us.' So, he gave them his attention, expecting to receive something from them. Then Peter said, 'silver and gold I do not have, but what I do have I give you: In the name of Jesus Christ of

Nazareth, rise up and walk.' And he took him by the right hand and lifted him up, and immediately his feet and ankle bones received strength. So, he, leaping up, stood and walked and entered the temple with them, walking, leaping, and praising God" (Acts 3:1–8).

I believe Peter and John had consistent prayer lives as they fellowshipped regularly with Father. As a result, a lame man was healed to not only walking but also jumping and leaping with praise and thanksgiving. Apparently, the man was brought to the gate daily to ask for handouts from those passing by. On this day, and at this appointed time, the man had a men-of-God, fellowship-with-God-walkers encounter. I believe, because of Peter and John's prayer life, they position themselves to hear from Holy Spirit, which resulted in the power of God to and through them to the man at the gate. A consistent prayer life walks hand in hand with fellowshipping with God. A vital component of fellowship with God is talking with Him. Prayer is communicating, not just asking God for stuff, but having intimate conversation.

When Peter and John (fellowshipping together) were heading to the place of prayer, they came across the man at the beautiful gate and because of their fellowship with God and one another, Peter asked the man at the gate to look upon them. Peter knew by Holy Spirit exactly what the man needed and exactly what to give him, and it was not money. In the Name of Jesus, Peter said, rise and walk. After the rulers, elders, and scribes got wind of this awesome healing of God by Peter and John they threaten them, but Peter and John preached the more with boldness, so much so, the scribes and rulers perceived that Peter and John were unlearned and ignorant men, they marveled and said they had been with Jesus (Acts 4:1–13). Men and women of God we are the arms of healing in our cities, as it was with Samuel, and Peter and John, it is to be with us, but it will require fellowship and not relationship only.

God has called and continues to call His people to spend more time before Him in prayer and fellowship, reading and meditating in His word. Doing so will sharpen our spiritual senses to hear Holy Spirit and discern His direction. We, too, can experience as Jesus experienced, to where we only do what we see our Father doing. Fellowship with God, by His Spirit, is where this will happen.

— *Chapter 15* —

WORSHIP AND PRAISE

s a little boy I liked the beats and the rhythm of those handclapping and foot-stomping songs that the saints of God sang and praised at the church my grandmother attended. Most of the time I paid little attention to the lyrics. Some twenty years later, after receiving Christ in my heart, not much changed initially, as I still attended more to the rhythm and beat more than the song itself.

I later noticed that the more I sought after and entered a deeper fellowship with God, the more I attended to the lyrics of songs song at church services. When I started focusing on the lyrics, I noticed some songs I enjoyed did not worship or praise Father God at all. Many of those songs focused on my circumstances or the problems and challenges I faced in life. I'm sure these were well meaning songs by the artists, but fellowship will change your heart, so much so that your desire will become a longing to know His heart and will. No, I will mention none of the songs here, as that is not my reason or purpose for saying this. There are many pleasant songs that are more self-centered than they are worshipful and praising to our Holy Father, YHWH God. We are called to worship Him in spirit and truth. Worshipping Him in spirit comes from a deep place of fellowship. In that place is where we become knowledgeable of what He has determined as worship to Him, and what manners of worship and praises pleases Him.

A local church or assembly that worships and praise Father God from a congregated pure heart receives manifestations of Him dwelling in the midst of their worship and praise. I believe God loves it when He is worshipped and praised for who He is, and not only for what He gives.

Psalmists, musicians, singers, I believe when you spend quality time in fellowship with Holy Spirit, He will tell you what to write. He will be your inspiration and from you will flow lyrics that destroy yokes and remove burdens from the lives of those the enemy has bound. Why? Because of anointed worship and praise. I would rather hear a person under the anointing that may not be the best singer or musician than hear a skilled singer and musician with no anointing. Fellowship with Holy Spirit brings with it the anointing to worship and praise yokes and burdens off people's lives.

From a life of fellowship with God, praise and worship is what I do because praise and worship is who I have become, as I present myself wholly and completely to Him.

A wonderful scripture I say every morning relative to praise is in the book of Jeremiah: "Heal me, O Lord, and I shall be healed; save me, and I shall be saved, for You are my praise" (Jer. 17:14). God is my praise, my tehillah, which is one of the Hebrew words for praise. Tehillah comes in the form of a hymn, song, laudation, or shout unto the Lord. God is my song. Fellowship with God will cause you to see God as your song! This along will make you shout unto the Lord the glory due to His name and worship the Lord in the beauty of holiness (Ps. 29:2).

Fellowship with God will cause you to make His praise glorious, declaring all the earth shall worship or bow before Him and sing praises to His Name (Ps. 66:1).

Fellowship with God will move a person into becoming what Jesus called a true worshipper, where they rise and worship the Heavenly Father in spirit and truth. God loves it when He is worshipped just because of who He is. I believe such worship brings Him (God) joy. It is the joy of the Lord (His joy) that strengthens the heart of the worshipper. (Read about this in John 4.)

— *Chapter 16* —

PAUL

*I*t has been attributed to Apostle Paul to have written several books in the New Testament. When I carefully read the books written by Paul, I see the concept of fellowship with God throughout.

Paul constantly used phrases like "know Him." "Know Him," in those instances, had fellowship in mind. Paul was not talking about knowing about God, as many with a relationship with God know about Him. Fellowship with God takes you from knowing about God to knowing Him. This knowing is intimacy, getting in close, so close you come to realize that in Him you live, move, and have your being.

In Philippians, Chapter 3, Paul, writing to the church at Philippi, said his desire was that he may know God and the power of His resurrection and the fellowship of his sufferings. Paul knew he would pay a price for serving Christ. He risked being persecuted and even being killed. He went into this fellowship with Christ with his eyes wide open. After all, Paul knew what persecution was all about. It was Paul that led the charge to persecute the church at its infancy, when it was getting started. Nevertheless, Paul was willing to endure what his walk, his knowing, his fellowship with Christ would bring, for he knew that the persecution he would encounter would not and could not come close to comparing with eternal living with Christ in His Kingdom. Fellowship with God will cause you to see your life in Christ beyond your life in the world. However, you see your life in the world as a life that glorifies God. Knowing God with the mindset of intimacy with Him will lead you to make Him known to others.

In Paul's first letter to the church at Corinth, he recognized the church had many teachers and instructors, but they did not have many fathers. Fathers fellowship. Fathers take time to mentor others. Paul had experience with this, as he mentored young Timothy. Paul saw Timothy as his spiritual son and friend. Good scriptures to study about this are 1 Corinthians 4:15, 1 Timothy 1, Acts 16 and Philippians 2. For Paul to see Timothy as his son, and Timothy to see Paul as his father, they had to have fellowship. This was not a mere acquaintance; this was so much more. In Paul's letters to Timothy, one time he addressed him as his "dearly beloved" son, and the other time he addressed him as his "own" son.

"Finally, brethren, farewell. Become complete. Be of good comfort, be of one mind, live in peace; and the God of love and peace will be with you. Greet one another with a holy kiss. All the saints greet you. The grace of the Lord Jesus Christ, and the love of God, and the communion of the Holy Spirit be with you all. Amen" (2 Cor. 13:11–14).

In the above scripture, Paul wrote to comfort and encourage the saints to commune with Holy Spirit. This phrase "communion of" Holy Spirit shows Paul's desire for the church at Corinth (and still for the children of God today) is to fellowship with Holy Spirit.

In Paul's letter to the church at Ephesus, he prayed and encouraged the saints there that they come to the fullness of knowing of their possessions in Christ. Paul knew if he could get the saints at Ephesus to realized how blessed it is to fellowship with God, by His Holy Spirit, that they would come to know what they possess in Christ, His power was at work in their lives to be all and to do all of what Christ wants, and that they would come to know of their inheritance in Christ, and that the Spirit of wisdom and understanding were available to them all. The key to all of this and more is fellowshipping with Holy Spirit. Holy Spirit is the One who receives from Jesus and makes all the things received known to the saints of God. You will be blessed to read and study this in John 16.

On one occasion when Paul was visiting Athens, he came across a marker with the inscription "the Unknown God." Well, this did not sit well with Paul. His spirit within him was provoked, so he used it as an opportunity to preach the gospel of the Kingdom. Here is the account:

"For as I was passing through and considering the objects of your worship, I even found an altar with this inscription: Therefore, the One whom you worship without knowing, Him I proclaim to you: God, who made the world and everything in it, since He is Lord of heaven and earth, does not dwell in temples made with hands. Nor is He worshiped with men's hands, as though He needed anything, since He gives to all life, breath, and all things" (Acts 17:23–25).

I imagine Paul was thinking, "You people are worshipping a God you call unknown. Let me introduce Him to you, for I know Him. He is the true and only God, the God that presence knocked me off my horse that day on Damascus Road. This is the same Paul who persecuted the saints of God before being touched by God and giving himself wholly to God. This same Paul endured much as he walked in close fellowship with God. In this same chapter 17 in the book of Acts, it is recorded that Paul was called a babbler. It was said that he spoke strange things to their ears. Yes, he did. Paul knew the people in Athens spent most of their time often talking about some new things or teachings that someone there had heard, so Paul used this opportunity to preach the kingdom of God, to include Jesus and His resurrection, with signs and wonders following.

Paul may have appeared to be a babbler to those that did not know God, but to God, Paul was a fellowship-walking son, who had become a powerful oracle of His.

— *Chapter 17* —

HOLY SPIRIT

However, when He, the Spirit of truth, has come, He will guide you into all truth; for He will not speak on His own authority, but whatever He hears He will speak; and He will tell you things to come. He will glorify Me, for He will take of what is Mine and declare it to you. All things that the Father has are Mine. Therefore, I said that He will take of Mine and declare it to you.

JOHN 16:13–14

Jesus tells His disciples that He was going away, that He would soon be crucified. After hearing this, His disciples' hearts became filled with sorrow. To comfort them, Jesus tells them that He will send them another comforter, Holy Spirit. He said that Holy Spirit was coming and would be to their benefit, and that Holy Spirit would teach them all things, even bring to their remembrance all the things Jesus had shared with them through their time of fellowship. The disciples were not trying to hear this, for they had come to love Christ with all their hearts. They just could not imagine the God of all, who became flesh and walked among His creation, who demonstrated His power and authority as He preached about the Kingdom of God, is now planning to give all that up and willingly submit to persecution and the cross. Jesus obviously knew the whole story. He came to earth to be the sacrifice to reconcile man back to God, his maker.

The disciples had much time fellowshipping with Jesus. Now they would learn that they still could fellowship with Christ. But now it will be by His Holy Spirit, whom Jesus called "Comforter." This Comforter came to do many things in and to the children of God. Three of the most wonderful things He has come to do is to reveal the secrets of God, the heart, and thoughts of God to those that will receive Him. (Read about this in 1 Corinthian 2.)

Holy Spirit also imparts gifts for ministry in each believer. These gifts are word of wisdom, word of knowledge, faith, gifts of healing, working of miracles, prophecy, discerning of spirits, divers kinds of tongues, and interpretation of tongues. All of which are listed in 1 Corinthians 12. Therefore, it is so important that we consistently fellowship with Holy Spirit. Fellowshipping with Holy Spirit is fellowshipping with Christ. Jesus said Holy Spirit will take of Him, Jesus and reveal or give what He receives to His children.

Habitation (Not Visit)

There is a difference between God, by His Spirit coming to visit me verses coming to habitat in me. My fellowship with Him has brought me to a place where I no longer pray for God's presence. I have come to know that His presence is always with me. I walk in His presence. Relationship thinking calls for His presence, fellowship-thinking walks in His presence.

God may manifest His presence in ways I sometimes feel and see the results of the manifestations, but the truth is His presence is always with us. You may ask, where was His presence when this happened or that happened. I remember when my wife and I got the message of the passing of our son, that news caused us to go through many emotions, thoughts, questions. Amid all our emotions, thoughts, feelings, confusions, and questions, one thing for certain was God's presence never left. Why? Because He came into our lives to habitat and not just visit. Consider this; you have a family member or friend that comes to visit you. When a family member or friend visited you, you were excited to see them. However, you knew when the person arrived that there would come a time, be it a few days or weeks, the person would eventually leave to go back to his or her own place. Well, I do not just want Holy Spirit to visit me. I want Him to stay and never leave. I think it is worth saying again, I do not have to pray for Holy Spirit's presence, I walk in His presence. Even when it does not feel like it, His presence is with me. Jesus promised He will never leave me nor forsake me. He kept that promise by imparting Holy Spirit in my life. This is the same Holy Spirit that hovered over the face of the waters during the creation of all things in the heavens and earth. He has been sent to hover over and abide in and upon me, and you, and to bring life to the purpose of God for me and you.

It is Holy Spirit who makes every scripture in the Bible come alive to everyone that opens their hearts to Him. Holy Spirit, as He habitat in me, gives me the logos (God's thoughts behind what He inspired men to write), and He sometimes gives a person a direct and specific spoken word (rhema) for a specific purpose and direction, like the time when the apostles were worshiping the Lord and fasting, when Holy Spirit spoke directly and said, separate unto me Barnabas and Saul for the work to which I have called them. (Acts 13:2) (Read the entire chapter, Acts 13.)

The greater works, the power, and the manifestation thereof that Jesus talks about in John 14 will come about through the lives of the men and women of God who fellowship with Him. In verse 23, of chapter 14, Jesus makes a fellowship statement when He said, if a person loves Him, that person will keep His (Jesus) word; and God will love him, and He and God will come to that person and make their (God and Jesus) home with that person.

Abide in Him

Holy Spirit's habitation is about Him abiding in me. Here I will share about abiding in Christ, through Holy Spirit.

Walking and living in the Spirit is about fellowship and character development. Holy Spirit hovers over my being with great anticipation to bring the work of God to fruition in and through me. Apostle Paul encourages us to know that we are the temple of God, and that the Spirit of God dwells in us (1 Cor. 3).

In John 15, Jesus told His disciples that the only way to bear fruit is to abide in the true vine (Him). Jesus, as gardener of my soul knows how and what to prune from me to make me as He wants me to be. Therefore, it is so important that I stay attached to the Vine (Jesus) and allow Holy Spirit to develop His character in me. I can't accomplish the works Jesus requires of me unless I abide in Him. Abiding in Him enables me to glorify God with my life. I come to know His purpose for my existence. I become knowledgeable of His thoughts on matters concerning me, and if He so chooses, of others for their benefit. I come to know what I can ask or call for according to His will, and for His pleasure. (Read and study Romans 12, 1 John 5, Philippians 2, and Hebrews 13.)

My actions are to be expressions of inward fellowship with God, so much so that I do not grieve Holy Spirit.

Anointing (or Anointed)

Anointing is the empowerment of Holy Spirit, the effective working of Holy Spirit in our lives.

God anoints a person for His purpose: to serve. It is the anointing that gives us the power to do what we have been called to do. Therefore, one should not become careless with the anointing of God on and in his or her life. The anointing is to be respected—it is from God. If a person doesn't respect the anointing, I believe that person will not receive all of what the anointing brings. This includes how a person receives from the anointing on another person's life. This could be leadership at a church, those God has placed over you in ministry. It is the anointing that takes burdens away and destroys yokes off people's lives. (Read Isaiah 10:27.)

Perhaps one reason the Church is not walking in all God would have it to walk in is because many in the Church do not cherish the anointing of Holy Spirit in and upon their lives.

Here are examples of where I see carelessness with the anointing:

Saul got careless with his position and authority (anointing). When Saul went up against the Amalekites, he was told to smite and destroy them all, and all their oxen, donkeys, camels, sheep—everything. He decided to spare Agag their king, the best of the sheep, oxen, fatlings, and lambs. His disobedience and lack of respect for the anointing on his life as king of Israel, which came with specific instructions from God through His prophet, Samuel, resulted in the Spirit of the Lord leaving Saul, and the kingdom to be stripped from him and given to David. (Read about this in 1 Samuel 16.)

Solomon got careless with the anointing as king. He loved what the scripture noted as many strange women, to include the daughter of Pharaoh. The Lord commanded the children of Israel not to enter marriage with the women of the other nations. The Lord knew if they did such that the other nations would cause them to turn their hearts from following Him (Father God) to the false gods of the other nations. Yep, it happened as God said. Solomon led by example—not the right example. Over time, when Solomon became old, his wives turned his heart to other gods and Solomon did evil in the sight of God. Solomon even built high places for the false gods Chemosh and Molech and allowed his many wives to burn incense and make sacrifices unto their gods. Well, God was not happy with Solomon. (Read and study 1 King 11.)

I see a valuable lesson here: Do not take the anointing in you for granted. The anointing is precious; treat it as such, embrace it. Fellowship with Holy Spirit will help the man or woman of God guard against this.

Chapter 18

SURRENDER

Surrendering in fellowship with Holy Spirit says, "Not my will Lord, your will be done." I exchange my will for God's will and desire for my life. My will becomes transformed as I conform to His will.

The Hebrew word Yadah means "praise." What's interesting is that Yadah means to lift extended hands. It also means "absolute surrender." Therefore, surrendering to God can be seen as a form of praise to Him.

Apostle Paul, in his letter to the church at Rome encouraged the saints then, and to the people of God now, to present themselves as living sacrifices. Surrendering oneself is totally up to the person. It must be done willingly. (See Romans 12.)

Holy Spirit has come to help the people of God give themselves to Him. It is Holy Spirit that enables us to give way to God's desire, relinquishing ownership of self. God gave man a will, and He wants man to willingly yield his will to His will for His glory.

Fellowship with Holy Spirit has brought me to where I rejoice knowing that my body is called a temple of God's Spirit, that He lives in me, and I am not my own, because I was bought with the price Jesus paid for with His blood on that cross. Therefore, I delight in honoring God with my body and spirit. I belong to Him (1 Cor. 6:19).

Apostle James wrote, "Submit to God, resist the devil and he will flee" (James 4:7–8). This is so important as when my heart and soul are focused on intimacy with God, from that place I am empowered to withstand all the devil send my way. Why? I see being in Christ to include whatever the enemy sends at me; he also sends at Christ. I rely on His power for my resisting the enemy. My unconditional surrender always works out for my good, as God knows what is best and right for me—much better than I do. So, I Yadah Him by complete surrender.

"Be clothed with humility, for "God resists the proud, but gives grace to the humble." Therefore, humble yourselves under the mighty hand of God, that He may exalt you in due time, casting all your care upon Him, for He cares for you". (1 Pet 5:5–7).

Many things are imparted and received from a humbled, low-lying position; visions, peace, strength, word of knowledge, just to name a few. I know a person can receive these while sitting or standing. However, I have experienced time and time again, hearing and seeing clearer when I am in the bowed or humbled position. Surrendering makes humility a beauty to behold. It starts in the hearts of the people of God.

With me, as my heart surrenders, my body follows, and this I have come to know, happens the more I fellowship with God.

—— Chapter 19 ——

CHURCH (EKKLESIA)

In Matthew 16, Jesus asked His disciples, who did the people say He was. Christ wanted to know what the disciples were hearing from the people in the towns they visited, about who the people said He was. The disciples told Jesus, some people said that He was John the Baptist, some said He was Elijah, and others said He was Jeremiah or one of the prophets. After hearing this, Jesus asked them who was He to them. I imagine Jesus thinking that these men had walked with Him, lived with Him, fellowshipped with Him, seen Him do miracles, and heard Him speak with authority and power, and He wanted to know what they thought about Him, who was He to them. Peter answered Jesus, and said, "You are the Christ (Messiah or Anointed One), the Son of the living God". (Mat 16:16)

Jesus's response to Peter was powerful. Jesus told Peter he was a blessed man, that the only way Peter could have gotten that revelation of who Jesus was it had to come from Father God.

"And I also say to you that you are Peter, and on this rock, I will build My church, and the gates of Hades shall not prevail against it. And I will give you the keys of the kingdom of heaven, and whatever you bind on earth will be bound in heaven, and whatever you loose on earth will be loosed in heaven" (Matt. 16:18–19).

Jesus knew that Peter's response did not come by any natural or human means, sensing that Peter received the revelation by word of knowledge given by Holy Spirit. Then Jesus said to Peter that He will build His church and the gates of hell (power of darkness) shall not prevail or triumph against or over it.

The Church has delegated responsibility and authority by the empowering of Holy Spirit to carry out God's purpose on the earth, amongst which is to pray corporately. When the Church gathers in corporate prayer, chains come off cities and towns. It is there where principalities and spiritual wickedness are challenged and defeated. As I stated under the section on prayer, fellowship will lead the Church into a more consistent prayer life.

The Church, as the body of Christ, must flow with the Head of the Church (Christ) for it to succeed at prevailing over the gates of hell. To flow with the Head, the church must consistently fellowship with Him. Otherwise, it will not accomplish all of what it has been built for.

God placed in His Church anointed officials, positions and giftings to help all members of the Church join in and administer the work of ministry, to serve God and each other as the Church go into all the earth preaching and teaching the Kingdom of God. (Read and study about the gifts and positions in 1 Corinthians 12 and Ephesians 4.)

"Behold, how good and how pleasant it is for brethren to dwell together in unity! For there the Lord commanded the blessing, life forevermore" (Ps. 133:1 and 3).

The word unity in this verse immediately brings to mind "fellowship." I believe God loves commanding blessings amid His people when they consistently fellowship with Him and with one another. Jesus promised the Church, the enemy cannot and will not prevail against it. The key, I believe, is fellowship. This is what the world needs to see, and will benefit by, the church filling the earth with the knowledge of the Glory of God by intimately walking hand in hand, step by step with its Builder, Jesus.

— Chapter 20 —

COMMUNITIES—GO YE!

hurch is to extend beyond the buildings and go into the communities. Communities are people. We must reach people with the Word and power of God, thereby glorifying Him. It is not about the building where the people gather. No, it is not about that. Jesus built His Church to reach communities with His love and grace. Fellowship with God makes it all about Christ and His influence in our communities by the power of His Word and Spirit.

"For the earth will be filled with the knowledge of the glory of the Lord, as the waters cover the sea" (Hab. 2:14).

One place the knowledge of the Glory of God is needed is in our communities. This can be accomplished by God's people fellowship-walking with His Spirit. It is Holy Spirit who expresses the heart of God through His people to our communities and cities. God's people are called to labor together with God. (Read about this in 1 Corinthians 3.)

The Church is a community established by God and placed on the earth to affect the communities of the world.

This is a sketch of something Holy Spirit impressed upon my heart about five years ago during a meeting with other saints at a weekend Bible study.

REACHING COMMUNITIES BY:

WORSHIPPING GOD

RECEIVING FROM GOD,

KNOW AND WALK-OUT WHO YOU ARE IN GOD

HUMBLING OURSELVES BEFORE GOD

What our communities need and will benefit by is His Church moving from relationship to fellowship with Him. This requires humbling ourselves, receiving of His Holy Spirit, worshipping and praising Him, and walking out who we are in Him. Our communities need to be impacted by great exploits at the hand of God through His people. People of God's primary goal should not be to just make it to heaven, but to receive heaven on earth, by allowing Holy Spirit to work the will of God in our lives. Fellowship-walking with Holy Spirit will bring this to being just like He did during the creation of the heavens and the earth in the very beginning. Apostle Paul makes it clear that it's God who works in His people both to will and to do for His good pleasure—His own delight (Phil. 2).

Consistent fellowship with Holy Spirit, you will know where to go in the communities, who to see in the communities, what to say and how to approach those you come in contact within your communities.

"I do not pray for these alone, but also for those who will believe in Me through their word; that they all may be one, as You, Father, are in Me, and I in You; that they also may be one in Us, that the world may believe that You sent Me. And the glory which You gave Me I have given them, that they may be one just as We are one: I in them, and You in Me; that they may be made perfect in one, and that the world may know that You have sent Me, and have loved them as You have loved Me" (John 17:20–23).

Apostles, prophets, evangelist, pastors, and teachers, when your fellowship with Holy Spirit is consistently happening, you will see results of this affecting your local congregations and communities.

Men and women of God, as you walk in fellowship with God, you present God to the communities and cities you live in. I know God is everywhere, as He is omnipresent, but He reveals Himself to communities and cities through His people. He has placed local assemblies in communities to point the citizens to Him.

God is looking for His people to walk by the power of His Spirit in our day, affecting communities like those that walked with Him in their generations. Moses, Job, Enoch, Samuel, Elijah, David, Paul, Peter, John all affected their generations by—you guessed it—fellowship. People of God in our generation can do the same.

When we fellowship with God by Holy Spirit, we bring the manifested presence of God in our communities and cities. It is God's manifested presence or glory that will change the spiritual climate of a meeting, a community, a city, a region, and a nation!

When we fellowship with God, we have access to the resources of God as King, and His Kingdom. In His Kingdom, our needs (whatever is needed to carry out His purpose) are given.

God's people are to be ambassadors of His Name and Word as He has given the Church the ministry of reconciliation. Love is the foundation of reconciliation, and God is Love. He does not just have love, He is Love. (Read and study about it in 2 Corinthians 5.)

Fellowship-walking with Holy Spirit will cause the love of God to saturate our hearts and express love to all people. After all, God has made from one blood every nation of men to dwell on all the face of the earth, and He has determined their pre-appointed times and the boundaries of their dwellings, so that they should seek Him, in the hope that they might grope or feel for Him and find Him, though He is not far from each one of us; for in Him we live and move and have our being, as also some of your own poets have said, "For we are also His offspring" (read and study Acts 17).

I visited a dear friend, Kelvin Steele, Pastor of ABBA Father Church. What a wonderful example of a church reaching the community where God has placed it. Pastor Steele and ABBA Father Church members do an annual "Spark in the Park" outreach. They had one of their outreaches during my visit. My experience with this outreach was heartwarming as I saw lives changed by the presence and power of God on that day in the park. I was moved by the church members giving of themselves, their love and joy in serving their community. You see, Pastor Steele and the members of ABBA Father Church are men and women in their city as Samuel was in the cities he visited. Pastor Steele saw that the harvest was plentiful, but the laborers were few, so he decided to not just pray that the Lord of the harvest would send out laborers into the harvest. Rather, he readied himself and his family and said, "Lord, send me. My family and I will go" (ref: Matt. 9:35–38).

Laborers in the kingdom of God go into the harvest and effectively affect the harvest from a place of fellowship. Fellowship will cause one not to un-righteously judge the harvest but go into the harvest with the heart of the One who sends him.

Note: I received Pastor Kelvin Steele's permission to mention him by name.

I believe the time is upon the people of God, more than ever, to make our God known to the world in ways that have not been known in our generations. We will be known as men and women of God in our communities and cities, primarily because of our intimate fellowship with God, by His

Spirit and our knowledge and application of His Word in our lives. Men and women of God will not just live in their cities; they will be God ambassadors in their cities and as such will draw attention to the reality of God and who He is.

— *Chapter 21* —

COVID-19

I n the years 2020 and 2021 when much news about the coronavirus were everywhere, Holy Spirit encouraged me to remain focused, rush nothing, and not for a moment take my heart's eye off my King and His Kingdom.

He also instructed me to observe those in the world and those in the Church. I admit, much of what I observed was quite interesting. But one thing is for sure: the virus in the land was and is another opportunity to see His Kingdom manifested in and through His people to the onlookers (those of the world and those in the spirit realm).

"If then, you were raised with Christ, seek those things which are above, where Christ is, sitting at the right hand of God. Set your mind on things above, not on things on the earth" (Col. 3:1–2).

To see the things in Christ, I must put my focus there. I must aim for and fix my thoughts on getting to know His heart and mind during this time and all times, so I know what to do during COVID-19. I believe, as the people of God fellowship with Holy Spirit, He will reveal insight and actions to be taken during this pandemic—what to do and what not to do and when to do what needs to be done. No, this has nothing to do with whether masks or gloves should be worn.

During the pandemic, I noticed how important fellowship was to people. Many complained about not being allowed to gather socially, whether to a sporting event, party, club, bar or visit family at hospitals. I believe what was being missed was fellowship. Fellowship is important to most, if not to all men, those in the Church and those outside the church.

— *Chapter 22* —

DREAMS

*D*reams (and/or visions) often communicates God's heart about matters of concern for a person or people. Dreams can draw a person to intimacy or fellowship with God—that's what dreams have done for me. Here are three dreams that communicated such to me. Apostle James said, "Draw nigh or near to God and He will draw nigh to you" (James 4:8).

Dream number 1: As a little boy around 8 or 9 years of age, I had this dream where I heard a voice say: come up here, I want to show you what I want you to do. I now know the voice I heard was the voice of my Father God. In the dream, God had called me unto Himself, which I now know was a call to fellowship. As a child, I did not know what to do with that dream, but when I became a man, and was born again, His Spirit brought the dream back to my remembrance. "Come up here," was God's call to me. I recall my focus was on the voice of Him who called me to come up. Obeying the call to come up to Him was on me, I had a choice. Choosing to heed

His voice positioned me to see and hear what He wanted to show me: fellowship.

Dream number 2: I had this dream in 1997. In this dream, I heard a voice say, "Son, look at them." Immediately this got my attention, however what I saw after hearing the voice say, "son look at them," was an old-styled mophead, the kind my Big Momma used. Now, that was a heavy-duty mop back then. I thought to myself, I do not see a "them," all I see is an old-style mophead. Then the voice became stronger and said, "Son, I said look at them." Then I looked directly and closer at the mophead. Then the voice said, "Do not you see how the threads of the mophead are intertwined with one another."

I answered, "Yes, I can see that."

Then the voice said, "That is how I see my people; many of them are intertwined with the things and ways of the world. I want you to know something about Me."

Right then is when, in the best way I can describe, a figure like unto a man appeared, but the figure appeared to be that of light and fire. This figure pulled my head toward the area of the figure liken unto a man's chest. The moment my head rested against what I describe as the heart area of a man's chest, I felt hurt and pain.

Then the voice said, "It hurts Me when My people, who are called by My Name, do and call things by My Name that I am not in the midst of."

The dream ended, and I came out of the dream crying and repenting, asking the Lord to forgive me for anything I done that added to the hurt and pain He felt. This changed my life and my walk with God, as I quickly realized the God of the universe, Creator of all things, that took on the form of man and came to earth to redeem man, this God has feelings. Then it dawned on me that He did create and made man in His image and likeness. Man has feelings, then it makes sense to me that my God has feelings. He cares about me and my life, and what I do as I fellowship-walk with Him. Fellowship!

Dream number 3: I had this dream about seven years ago. In this dream, I was standing at a gas station when my immediate attention was drawn to a group of people (some standing and some sitting) at what appeared to be a bus stop waiting for transportation. As I looked upon them, I declared (preaching in a rapping or poetic sort) to them the Gospel of the Kingdom of God; the good news that Jesus the Christ came to the earth in bodily form, and gave His life for us, and that salvation can only come through Him. Then I turned to my right, where my attention was drawn to the side of the gas station. To my left, as I faced the gas station building, to the left of the gas station, it appeared to become like a seashore, water rushing ashore. I then heard a voice say, "The land has been invaded. Come with me. Come to the place where I will reveal to you all you will need to recover the land, your land. I will give you instructions."

Then I saw myself and another man being led to an office where we were instructed to sit at an already-prepared table for us to receive from the One who called us to come with Him.

Holy Spirit revealed that the two men in the dream represented the offices of the apostle and prophet. He informed me that the church has been trying to fulfill its purpose with three (the pastor, teacher, and evangelist) of the five offices identified in Ephesians 5:11–12. Holy Spirit brought this back to my remembrance and told me the church at large is still trying to accomplish its God given purpose with an incomplete fold. There are many in the Church that think the apostle and prophet offices have been done away with. I believe scripture states otherwise. If Jesus put them in the church and the church is still active, then all the offices are to still be active. A problem has been the use of the offices, and gifts by some which have caused some to not want to have people that believe they are anointed in this way to be a part of their ministries. Unfortunately, there have been apostles and prophets who misused these offices. Likewise, there have been pastors, teachers, and evangelists who have misused their offices. Whether a person misuse or abuse an office or ministry does not mean God has ended that office. There are many apostles, prophets, teachers, pastors, and evangelist that truly live out their office for and to the Glory of God.

The apostle and prophet in my dream were already in a relationship with God. He was calling them into a place of fellowship; the place already prepared for them to meet with Him, to sit with Him, to dine with Him. From that place of fellowship, the apostle, prophet, teacher, pastor, and evangelist will receive directions, instructions, revelations on what to do regarding what has come and will come upon the land, their land.

The enemy has invaded the land, and the Church has a responsibility. That responsibility is not to run from it but to be the Church in it. When the Church corporately yields to the work of Holy Spirit, the Church will work the greater works on the earth, bringing heaven and earth together, and effectively deal with the invaders in the land.

I have inquired of the Lord, and was instructed to blow the trumpet in Zion, and tell the Church to pursue and over-take the invaders. God has given delegated authority to fulfill its (the Church) purpose for being built. This is to be done through fellowship-walking with God by His Holy Spirit.

When invited to come to the dinner table where the meal is already prepared, all needed at that point is to eat or par-take. Partake has the concept of fellowship.

Dream number 4: I had this dream about six years ago. In the dream I saw the earth round like a globe. From within or inside the heart of the earth rose a long table. As the table cleared, the surface figures of men appear around the table. I remember there were several men at the table. All the men faced the direction of one man, looking intently and with an-ticipation to hear what the man they had focused on would say. I inquired of the Lord as to the meaning of the dream and was told "the man all the other men were looking in-tently to was Christ. The men were looking for directions on what to do on the earth, what to tell others about a kingdom that is not of this world and yet in this world.

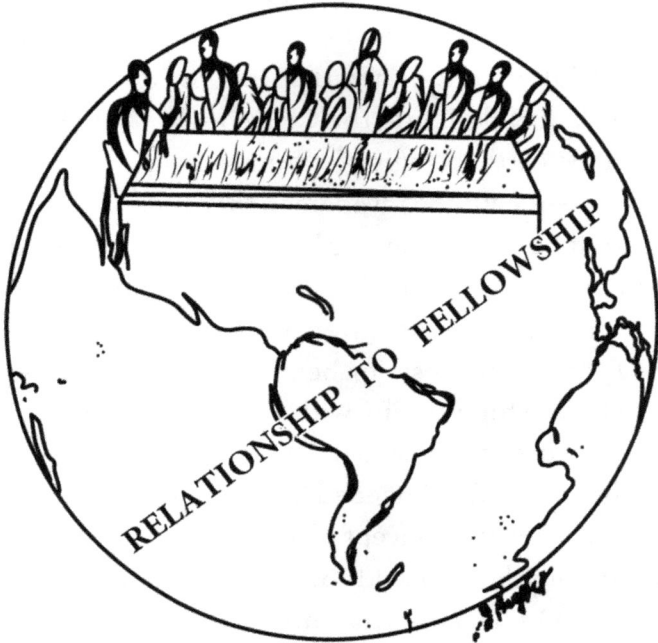

All these dreams, though different, had one key pull on my heart. Yes, it is fellowship! As a little boy, the dream to come up here was meant for me to come to fellowship with God. The dream about the old style mophead communicated intertwined with the Spirit of God, then I will learn God's heart, His will, and thoughts on matters in my life and the life of others. Dream about the invaders communicated intimacy with God brings insight into the enemies' plans and how to overcome such. The dream about the table and men risen from the earth communicated the same as the dream about the invaders, the only way to effectively deal with the many issues on the earth and administer from the kingdom of God to the earth is to focus on Jesus. Seek first the kingdom of God (Jesus is King) and His righteousness and all the things will be added (things needed to fulfill your God given purpose). Fellowship is key!

Wonderful dream noted: it was by dreams to Joseph (Mary's husband) he received guidance and direction about what to do regarding the virgin, Mary's pregnancy before he and Mary were married and the name the child would be given, where to take Mary and the child after learning Herod sought to find and have the child killed. Of course, we know the child (Jesus or Yahshua) Mary conceived was of Holy Spirit. It was through dreams Joseph received what to do, when to do it, and where to go. (Read the book of Matthew, chapters 1 and 2)

I share more on dreams and visions in my book *Holy Spirit—Alpha and Omega*.

SUMMARY POINTS

Holy Spirit has come to God's creation (man) that man might come back to fellowship with Him. It is Holy Spirit who takes what is of Jesus and present those things He receives to God's people, the Church.

Fellowship with God gives me an opportunity to consistently hear His voice.

Manifesting the fruit of the Spirit (divine character/ nature) comes from fellowship.

Becoming a living epistle (word in me/me in the Word) comes from fellowship.

Fellowship is by faith.

As with Adam/Eve, Yahweh's desire was for man to fellowship by abiding in His manifested presence!

Manifesting His kingdom can be done by fellowshipping as we abide in His presence.

Manifesting His ways, actions, and character comes by abiding in His presence and fellowshipping.

Revelation comes from abiding/living in His presence. But some say the Bible is all the revelation we need, there is no other revelation. Apostles did not believe that!

Abiding in His presence and fellowshipping His laws/ ways are written in my heart.

Abiding in His presence and fellowshipping I become more sensitive to His voice in my spirit, and in dreams and visions.

Abiding in His presence and fellowshipping comes word of knowledge/wisdom, and ability to discern spirits.

Abiding in His presence and fellowshipping comes the authority and power to cast out devils, lay hands on the sick, preach deliverance to the captives, and give good news to the poor.

Abiding in His presence and fellowshipping He will show me hidden/secret things, things to come.

Restoration of fellowship, like the fellowship Adam and Eve had with Yahweh from the very beginning, I believe is included in this Scripture "and that He (God) may send Jesus Christ, who was preached to you before, who heaven must receive until the times of restoration of all things which God has spoken by the mouth of all his holy prophets since the world began". (Acts 3:20-21)

GLOSSARY

Church: (Greek, *ekklesia* which comes from two words *ek* meaning "out," and *kaleo*, meaning "to call.") In the classical Greek language prior to the Roman Empire, *ekklesia* meant "an assembly of citizens summoned by the crier, the legislative assembly."

Fellowship: (Hebrew/Greek): Communion, sharing in common, communication, contribution (what am I contributing to relationship), partner or partaker, companion or companionship.

Fellowship: (Greek, *koinonia*, pronounced "koy-nohnee'-ah"): partnership that is participation, to communicate or communication, communion, contribution. (Hebrew *chabar* pronounced "khaw-bar'): to join, join (together), have fellowship.

Focus: To converge on or toward a central point (our central point is always Christ. Jesus, you are the center of my joy, my peace, strength, life); to adjust one's vision so as to render a clear, distinct thought image (our vision or our seeing should always be through His Eyes, the eye of His

Spirit); to concentrate attention or energy (our concentrated attention must be in/to Christ).

Glory: manifested grace and power, character (His character in/through surrendered and yielded vessels). I must become such to give such! He is Father/ source of Glory.

Kabod (kaw bode'): "weight (figuratively), splendor, honor, weightiness" or "substance."

Doxa: honor, praise, worship, dignity.

Shekinah: A Hebrew word that refers to the manifest presence of God. When King Solomon had finished having the Temple of God built the presence of God came upon the Temple so powerfully "That the priests could not continue ministering because of the cloud; for the glory of the LORD filled the house of the lord" (1 King 8:11).

God: YHVW, YHWH, Yahweh, Yehovah, Jehovah, Elohim

Intimacy: Close familiarity or friendship; closeness. "The intimacy between a husband and wife," closeness, togetherness.

Intimate relationship: an interpersonal relationship that involves physical or emotional intimacy. Although an intimate relationship is commonly a sexual relationship, it may also be a non-sexual relationship involving family, friends, or acquaintances.

Relationship: (Free Dictionary): the condition or fact of being related; connection or association (as in blood or marriage; kinship).

Relative: 1) a person connected with another or others by blood or marriage. 2) something or someone having, or standing in, some relation or connection to something or someone else. 3) existing or having its specific nature only by relation to something or someone else; not absolute or independent.

Walk: (*Stoichos* in Hebrew): to walk in relation to others; walk in line, keep in step with, unity, harmony

ABOUT THE AUTHOR

Johnnie Prophet, raised in Miami, Florida, is married to his wife Jerlyn of 42 years. He is retired military "United States Air Force" after 22 years. While in the military, in 1992, he received the call to minister the gospel. He has served faithfully in positions as usher, deacon, elder, associate Pastor, Pastor, and presently serves as a presbytery member at House of Faith Church, Hudson Florida.

Johnnie Prophet recently launched Relationship to Fellowship Ministries. He conducts Holy Spirit Relationship to Fellowship workshops at no cost to the attendees.

Outreach ministries served: homeless, juvenile detention, men's shelters, and prison ministry. He believes God's people are anointed by Holy Spirit to preach good news to the poor, healing to the brokenhearted, liberty to the captives, recovery of sight to the blind, liberty to the oppressed, and to proclaim the favor of the Lord". (Luke 4:18-19).